RE Ideas: Fairness and Justice

The blatant unfairness of life is not a new phenomenon – it is a truth that has been grappled with over many centuries. Pupils are engaged by RE that seems relevant in contemporary life. Fairness and justice are real problems in practical terms, and religions and worldviews not only teach about this but encourage religious believers to act justly and fairly through practices and a call to action. It is for this reason that very often pupils find teaching about fairness and justice engaging and stimulating. Many agreed syllabuses and guidelines have outcomes for pupils around beliefs into action or aims that suggest pupils should 'express with increasing discernment their personal reflections and critical responses to questions and teachings about identity, diversity, meaning and value, including ethical issues.'

This book offers a whole school focus on the concepts of fairness and justice. For the youngest pupils we explore what is and isn't fair through pupil art and stories that are shared by Christians, Jewish people and Muslims, a story from the New Testament and a story from Sikhism. There are three units for older pupils that each take a single religion and look at the religion's response to ideas of fairness and justice. In the unit on Judaism we explore the Jewish concept of *tikkun olam*, healing the world, looking at acts of loving kindness, justice and the festival of Tu B'shevat. The practice of giving Zakat is the focus in our unit on Islam through a mystery strategy exploring this practice and the reality of this giving of alms in the life of a Muslim woman. Finally there are excellent links to discussion and debate in the English curriculum and to art in our unit on the Beatitudes of Jesus.

Fiona Moss
Editor

Support material on the RE Today website

The RE Today website offers NATRE members and RE Today subscribers some free additional resources and classroom-ready materials related to this publication. Look out for the 'RE Today on the web' logo at the start of selected articles.

The password for access can be found in each term's *REtoday* magazine or you can use your member/subscriber number.

www.retoday.org.uk

Age focus	Contents	Page
4–6	**What is fair?** Fiona Moss	2–6
5–7	**What do religions teach about fairness?** Stephen Pett and Julia Diamond-Conway	7–12
7–9	**How do Jewish people think we can 'mend the world'?** Stephen Pett	13–18
8–11	**Why does Zara give money away at Ramadan?** Fiona Moss	19–24
9–11	**Eight sentences for a happy world: the Beatitudes of Jesus** Lat Blaylock	25–30
Subject leader	**Fairness and justice: further ideas** Fiona Moss	31
Subject leader	**Fairness and justice: quotes from sacred text, sources of authority and inspirational people** Fiona Moss	32–33

Our writers and editors are alert to the differences between levels in the four nations of the UK. Our levelled outcomes can be adapted by teachers in their situations, taking account of the Core Syllabus, Religious Education (Northern Ireland) and the National Exemplar Framework for Religious Education, Wales. Specific reference has been made to the outcomes from the Scottish Curriculum for Excellence.

What is fair?

4–6

Background knowledge for teachers

Very young children can often have a heightened sense of what they consider to be fair or unfair. This unit acts an introduction to fairness, using a story that is shared in three religions. King Solomon and the story of his wisdom is to be found in the sacred texts of Christians, Jewish people and Muslims. In Islam King Solomon is referred to as Suleman.

This unit uses play-based ideas, art and storytelling to introduce the idea of fairness. It goes on to look at the idea of the Golden Rule, the one rule that religious and non-religious people all share and agree on: 'Treat other people as you would like them to treat you.'

There is further work on the Golden Rule in the unit for 5–7 year olds.

Essential knowledge for pupils

Pupils should know:

- the one rule that religious and non-religious people all share and agree on 'Treat other people as you would like them to treat you.'
- the story of King Solomon and what a meaning of the story is
- that the story of King Solomon is important to Christian, Jewish and Muslim people.

Web support

Subscribers and NATRE members can also download the following from the RE Today website: www.retoday.org.uk

- A PowerPoint presentation to support teachers with this unit.
- Further examples of artwork on the Golden Rule can be found in the 2014 Spirited Arts section of the NATRE website: **See:** www.natre.org.uk

Assessment for Learning

This section shows some of the outcomes achievable by pupils of different abilities in the 4–6 age range.

Level	Description of achievement: I can …
ELGs Almost all pupils in this age group	• have a developing awareness of my own needs, views and feelings and be sensitive to those of others • answer 'how' and 'why' questions about my experiences and in response to stories • listen to stories and guess what is going to happen • use talk to organise, sequence and clarify thinking, ideas, feelings and events.
1 Many pupils in this age group	• talk about what happened in the story of King Solomon in simple terms • say what the Golden Rule is • say what I think is good about sharing things fairly • share why you think some people say King Solomon was wise • share my own ideas about the Golden Rule.

This unit helps pupils in Scotland to achieve RME 0-02a, RME 0-05a and RME 0-09a.

Note: The levels used in the Assessment for Learning boxes have been derived from the 2004 *Non-statutory National Framework for RE*. These are found extensively in agreed syllabuses in England, but teachers are advised to consult the statutory requirements applicable to their school.

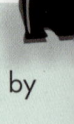

Activity 1: Human voting - fair or unfair

This activity is designed to help children realise that what is fair and what is unfair aren't always easy questions to answer.

Create four chalk or rope circles on the floor. Label them: completely fair, quite fair, completely unfair, quite unfair.

Explain to the children that you are going to read out a situation, then they can decide with a talk partner how fair or unfair they think it is and why, and then they must go and stand in the relevant circle.

Read out the situations on p.4. Ask some of the children to explain their choice. You could photograph their human voting for display. Older children could also suggest how to make the unfair situations more fair.

Arrange the class into four groups and ask them to create a picture of a completely fair, quite fair, completely unfair, quite unfair situation.

Activity 3: Playful learning

Leave the King Solomon story pictures and props available for play-based learning. Encourage children to retell the story, but also invite them to bring other problem scenarios for King Solomon to pronounce solutions for.

Activity 2: Acting out and interpreting a story

Sit the children down ready to share the story on p.5. Enlarge the five pictures of the story or use the PowerPoint available to members.

Show the children five items: a crown, a sword, a baby, and two women's scarves. Ask the children what the story might be about. Take suggestions and then place the crown on a child's head and declare him to be King Solomon.

Read part 1 of the story and show the picture. Ask the children to discuss in pairs:

- What does being wise mean?
- Who do you think is wise?
- What wise things might a king have to do?

Read part 2 of the story and show the picture. Choose two children to wear the scarves and join Solomon to help you tell the story.

After you have told part 2 of the story arrange the children into groups of three and ask them to act out what happens next. What will King Solomon say? How will the women react? Give each group of three a scroll of paper to draw and/or write what King Solomon should do. After each group has acted out their scenario, share the scenarios with the class and get them to deliver the scrolls to you with suitable dramatic style. You could even place the crown on your head and act the role of King Solomon reading their suggestions.

Read part 3 of the story and show the picture. Ask the children to discuss in pairs:

- What do you think the women said?
- Was King Solomon's idea fair or unfair?
- Was this a wise thing for him to say?

Read part 4 of the story and show the picture. Choose seven children and create a 'Conscience Alley' at the front of the class. Choose one child to act as King Solomon. Place three children on his left in a line, facing inwards. Place three children on his right in a line, facing inwards, creating a corridor for Solomon to step into. The children on the left offer a reason why he should not use the sword, the children on the right offer a reason why he should use the sword. At the end, ask the child playing Solomon what his decision is and why.

Share the end of the story and the picture.

RE Today Services

Fair – unfair – quite fair – quite unfair

Elsie's mum is quite poorly so Elsie can't always come to Rainbows.

Oliver and George are brothers. Oliver loves spaghetti bolognese but George doesn't like it that much. Every Tuesday Dad makes spaghetti bolognese.

Ruth is very busy playing with the LEGO®. She is using all the windows to build a house. Ahmed comes to play with the LEGO® but Ruth doesn't notice because she is so busy building her house. Ahmed can't build a house because there are no windows left.

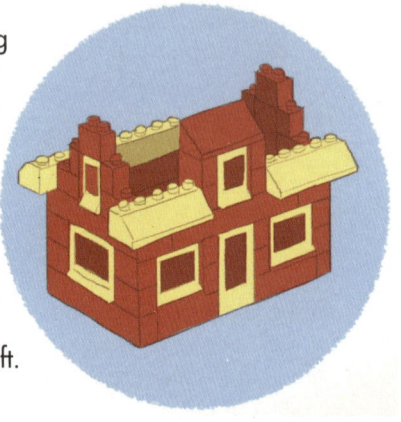

There are two chocolate cakes in the fridge. They are exactly the same. One belongs to you and one to your friend. When you take them out to eat, one has gone mouldy and it can't be eaten. Your mum splits the cake that is left so you each get half.

You love playing football. Your uncle has bought you a new football for your birthday but you find out that it was made by a boy who was only seven. He has to work so hard he can't go to school.

In some places people get teased because of the religion they belong to or the colour of their skin.

James always gets something different in his packed lunch but you always get the same old sandwiches.

Puja is very sad every day when she comes to school. She always cries when her mum leaves her so she gets to sit near the teacher on the carpet at the beginning of every day.

King Solomon the wise

You might know the story of brave David who fought Goliath and went on to become a king. Well this is the story of one of his sons – Solomon.

1 King David was known for his bravery and for following God. When Solomon became king he prayed to God to give him wisdom to be a good and fair king.

2 Two women came to see the king; one of them was holding a baby. One woman was crying, 'This woman stole my baby. Her baby died and while I was sleeping she took my healthy baby and gave me the baby that had died.'

3 What do you think King Solomon did? He sent for a sword and said, 'Cut the baby in half! Give each woman half of it.'

4 Immediately the woman who said her baby had been stolen shouted, 'Stop! Let her have the baby. Don't kill the child.' But the other woman said, 'You are right, Great King, neither of us should have the baby – use the sword.'

5 King Solomon smiled – this was exactly what he thought would happen. 'Give the baby to the first woman: she is its real mother. She would rather give away her baby than see it hurt.'

The people were pleased that God had given King Solomon the wisdom to be fair.

Artistic interpretations of the Golden Rule

Activity 4: The Golden Rule

Prepare a golden box. In the golden box place a scroll on which you have written the Golden Rule: 'Treat other people as you would like them to treat you.' With suitable drama, share with the children that there is one rule that both non-religious people and religious people share; some say it is the most important rule. Reveal and read the scroll.

Discuss with the children what the rule means and what life would be like if people followed the rule.

In 2014 the NATRE Spirited Arts competition had 'The Golden Rule' as a category. Share with pupils some of the entries shown on this page. There are further entries at www.natre.org.uk/about-natre/projects/spirited-arts

Set the children an artistic challenge. Can they create a picture that shows the Golden Rule being followed and either write or explain what their picture is about? You could have a mini class competition, or alternatively create a group artistic representation of the Golden Rule.

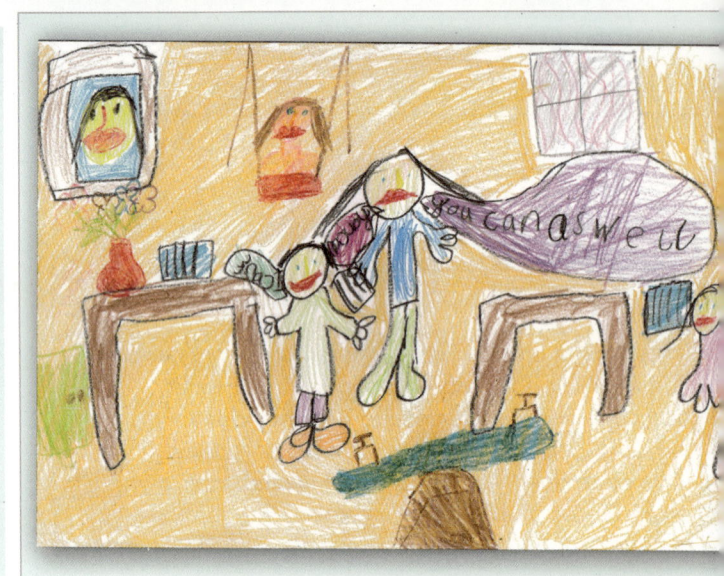

'This is a little boy who says, "I can't do it." Then this is me saying "Yes you can," because I want to be an encourager. I want to teach people how to do science so they can make medicines and if someone has an infection they can give the medicine.'

Mariam, 6

In my picture you can see ....
help in sumbode up
Freddie

No Matter What's the Weather

'I want to be a kind person. In my picture there is sunshine and rain. The picture shows people still helping in the good times and the bad times.'

Grace,

What do religions teach about fairness?

5–7

Background knowledge for teachers

Most young children have a sense of fairness and justice, even if it is based upon getting upset if someone else gets something and they don't. This series of activities explores the idea of fairness a little more deeply, making links between their own experiences and then looking at the Golden Rule, the idea of treating others as you would want to be treated.

The idea of fairness is then extended to look at forgiveness, using Jesus' story of the Unforgiving Servant as a way in. Forgiveness is a stage on from fairness; you might say that it is not fair to forgive someone a debt that they owe, whether financial (as in the story) or because they have hurt you. However, many religions teach that forgiveness is necessary, both for the person doing the forgiving as well as the person forgiven.

This story is a good background to the more well-known parable of the Forgiving Father (otherwise known as the Lost or Prodigal Son). Christians believe that God forgives and forgets, and welcomes sinful people when they turn back to him.

The unit then explores a lovely story from Sikhism that encourages more fairness, asking children to consider whether there is room for more fairness, goodness and kindness in the world before exploring the meaning of forgiveness further through the Jewish story of Jonah. Finally, pupils are encouraged to compare and contrast messages from the stories.

You may decide to use all three stories or just to use two of the stories, depending on the religions you focus on with your pupils.

Essential knowledge for pupils

Pupils should know:

- that fairness includes treating people equally
- that the Golden Rule is found in Jesus' teaching as well as in many other religions and is shared by many who are not religious.
- that forgiveness is important in Christianity and in life
- that Sikhism and Judaism (like other religions) want people to be kind, fair and forgiving.

Assessment for Learning

This section shows some of the outcomes achievable by pupils of different abilities in the 5–7 age range.

Level	Description of achievement: I can ...
1 Almost all pupils in this age group	• talk about what is fair and what is not fair • say what the Golden Rule is and give an example from my own life • recall elements of 'The Unforgiving Servant', 'The Milk and the Jasmine Flower' or 'Jonah and the Big Fish' • talk about things in the world that I am thankful for.
2 Many pupils in this age group	• talk about what happened in the story of The Unforgiving Servant, The Milk and the Jasmine Flower, or Jonah and the Big Fish • talk about why it is good to forgive people • begin to share the meaning of stories and say where they have similarities • talk about why Jews and Christians think it is important to forgive, and connect this to kindness and forgiveness in my own life.
3 The most able pupils in this age group	• describe what the Golden Rule and Jesus' story say about fairness and forgiveness • after thinking about Jesus' teaching, suggest ways in which it helps people to be kind and forgiving • describe what the story of Jonah teaches Jewish people about forgiveness.

This unit helps pupils in Scotland to achieve RME 1-02b and RME 1-05a.

Web support

Subscribers and NATRE members can also download the following from the RE Today website: www.retoday.org.uk

- The three stories from pp.10–12
- Additional strategies and samples of pupils' work from The Milk and the Jasmine Flower story.

RE Today Services

Activity 1 — Her piece is bigger than mine!

Either bring in a cake, if your Healthy School policy will allow it, or use a picture of a cake cut unevenly into larger and smaller slices.

Show it to your children and ask them to think which piece they would take (if it were real).

Ask some to reveal their choice. How many chose the biggest piece?!

Talk about that together. Is it good or right? What is the word you use when things are not shared equally …? Unfair? What does it mean to be fair? Share out the cake!

Can children think of some other examples of fairness or unfairness, where things are equal or unequal?

Activity 2 — The Golden Rule: making you think about fairness

One way of being fair comes from one of the teachings of Jesus. He teaches that people should treat others as they would like to be treated (Matthew 7:12). All of the world religions have a version of this teaching – it is often called the Golden Rule.

Ask the children to act out some scenes where people do not obey the Golden Rule:

- Someone has some sweets (healthy ones, of course) and refuses to share.
- Someone pushes others out of the way to get to the front of the queue.
- Some children whisper about another child and laugh about her.
- A child leaves all his stuff on the living room floor for his mum to clear up.

How do they feel when they are not treated fairly? What would be different if everyone obeyed the Golden Rule?

Activity 3 — Is forgiveness fair? The story of the Unforgiving Servant

Jesus told some stories about fairness, but he went a step further to show that forgiveness is better. The story of the Unforgiving Servant sets up some clear moments when children can say what they think the fair thing to do is, and also about what it means to forgive and be forgiven.

Read the story of the Unforgiving Servant on p.10 (Matthew 18:21-35). Stop at the points indicated and ask the questions.

Use ways of bringing the story alive to the children, such as by acting it out. You might freeze-frame the story and ask the children how the different characters feel at different points. You might give a child something heavy to hold for a while, then take it away – what does it feel like to have a heavy burden and have it taken away? Compare with the servant who owes such a lot and is forgiven.

The difficult last verses of the story show that it is really important for Christians to forgive if they expect God to forgive them! Note that Jesus seems to be saying that it is not good to try and get even. People should be forgiving. Forgiveness is not fair, exactly – it goes beyond fairness by not looking to get back at someone – so it is kind and loving.

Activity 4 — Applying the story

At the start of the story, Peter asks Jesus: 'Lord, if my brother keeps on sinning against me, how many times do I have to forgive him? Seven times?'

Ask children: What do you think Jesus said?

He said: 'Not seven times but seventy times seven!'

Talk about this with your children. See if you can get together 70 x 7 beads or counters and lay them out on a table. What would this be like? Do you think Jesus meant people should keep a count of how many times they have forgiven someone? Or is he saying, keep on forgiving – there's no limit!

Children may not think that they have things to forgive, particularly, but they can always be more kind. Thinking back to the Golden Rule, ask children to think of as many ways of being kind as they can. Put up a display with 490 dots, with some of them labelled with the kind things children can do.

RE Today Services

Activity 5: Learning from Sikhism

'The Milk and the Jasmine Flower' is a lovely story about Guru Nanak and how there is always room in the world for more fairness, peace and justice. Read through the story (p.11). Have a bowl of milk (or water) and a flower to illustrate the story. Talk about what the children think Guru Nanak might do when the messengers arrive. What do they think about how he used the jasmine flower? Why did Guru Nanak not just march into the city?

Ask your class to think of lots of things that we need more of in the world today. 'There's always room for more …'

Thank you to Sallie Boyd at Sutton Veny Primary School in Wiltshire for this idea. NATRE members and RE Today subscribers can download an article describing how she used this idea with older pupils.

Activity 6: Jonah and forgiveness

In the Jewish tradition, the story of Jonah is read on Yom Kippur – a day when Jews ask for forgiveness of their sins.

Read through the story on p.12, in an interactive manner. Perhaps allow children to sit in the shape of a boat or fish rather than the usual circle and give each child a percussion instrument. Stop the story at appropriate points to ask how characters might be feeling, what the atmosphere would be like or what is happening – discuss suitable responses and pupils can show these using their instruments.

Through class discussion and talk partners, pupils explore:

- Why do you think Jonah prayed in the fish?
- If Jonah didn't go to Nineveh the first time, why did he go on the second?
- Why did God keep Nineveh safe?
- Who was forgiven in this story?

At the Jewish ceremony of tashlich, Jews symbolically cast off sins by emptying their pockets into flowing water. Can children think of a time when they have needed to say sorry and/or be forgiven? Write or draw the incident onto the side of a small paper boat. Use the water tray to allow children to launch their boats and watch these incidents they are sorry for float away. If children cannot think of an example, you could have a list of generic examples and children choose the one they would like to see less of in the world to place on their boat.

Activity 7: Doing the right thing

Help pupils to compare the stories that they have heard in this unit. Put a hoop on the floor to represent each story. Support pupils in identifying the main messages behind each story, for example the importance of being fair, being good, being kind, being forgiving and showing that you are sorry. As pupils pinpoint each main message, write it on a slip of card and put it into the hoop for the corresponding story. Discuss with pupils which messages fit into more than one hoop, helping them to understand similarities between the stories.

Allow pupils time to demonstrate independently their understanding of similarities between the stories. This could be done in a number of ways, such as a piece of artwork with an oral explanation or an information poster.

The Forgiving King and the Unforgiving Servant

Jesus' friend Peter asked him how often he was supposed to forgive someone if they did something wrong. Jesus told this story:

The kingdom of heaven is like this. Once there was a king who decided to check on his servants' accounts. He had just begun to do so when one of them was brought in who owed him millions of pounds. The servant did not have enough to pay his debt.

Pause: What should the king do? What would be fair? Why?

The king ordered him to be sold as a slave, with his wife and his children and all that he had, in order to pay the debt.

Pause: Is this fair? Why/why not? What do you think the servant will do?

The servant fell on his knees before the king. 'Be patient with me,' he begged, 'and I will pay you everything!' The king felt sorry for him, so he forgave him the debt and let him go.

Pause: How did the man feel? Why?

Then the man went out and met one of his fellow servants who owed him a few pounds.

Pause: What do you think he will do?

The forgiven servant grabbed the one who owed him a few pounds and started choking him. 'Pay back what you owe me!' he said.

Pause: Is this fair? Why/why not? What do you think he should do?

His fellow servant fell down and begged him, 'Be patient with me, and I will pay you back!' But he refused; instead, he had him thrown into jail until he should pay the debt.

Pause: Is this fair? How does the servant feel?

When the other servants saw what had happened, they were very upset and went to the king and told him everything.

Pause: What do you think the king will do?

So the king called the servant in. 'You worthless slave!' he said. 'I forgave you the whole amount you owed me, just because you asked me to. You should have had mercy on your fellow servant, just as I had mercy on you.' The king was very angry, and he sent the servant to jail to be punished until he had paid back the whole amount.

Pause: Is this fair? What should the servant have done? Why?

And Jesus said, 'That is how my Father in heaven will treat every one of you unless you forgive your brother from your heart.'

Pause: Christians say that this means that it is really important to forgive, even if someone upsets you.

Matthew 18:21-35, Good News Translation

The Milk and the Jasmine Flower

Guru Nanak believed that everyone is equal. Rich or poor, sad or happy, brainy or practical: God sees everyone equally.

Five hundred years ago, Guru Nanak and his friend Mardana were travelling to a new city in India. He was such a famous holy man that the news about his arrival spread, and before he even got to the city gates, the holy men who lived in the city were talking about him.

They were worried!

They knew Guru Nanak was a truly good and holy person, and they had promised to try to be good like him. But they had actually been greedy and unkind. They were scared of Guru Nanak's arrival. He might show them up!

They decided to send a messenger with a bowl full of milk as a gift to say that there was no room for anyone else in the city: as the bowl was full, so was the city, and they were sorry that they could not receive Guru Nanak and Mardana. Please would the Guru and his companion go somewhere else?

As Guru Nanak walked up the road to the city gates, the messengers met him, carrying the gift of a large bowl, full to the brim with fresh milk.

'Our holy men send you this milk, and apologise that they cannot receive you,' said the messengers. 'Our city is already too full of holy men. You could go somewhere else.'

Nanak sat down with the messengers and the bowl.

Before he drank any, he picked a jasmine flower from a wayside bush and floated it on the top of the milk. Not a drop spilled out.

He looked around the group before he spoke, with a smile: 'I think the city is not quite full,' he said. 'As the flower finds space in the full bowl of milk, so there is always room for more holiness in the world.' The flower floated on top of the milk and not a drop was spilt: there was room for it!

The messengers went back into the city and told the holy men what had happened. They suddenly saw how silly they had been and felt sorry that they had tried to send Guru Nanak and Mardana away. They threw open the city gates and asked Guru Nanak and Mardana to stay with them and teach them how to fill their city with good things.

Jonah and the Big Fish

Long, long ago, there lived a man. A very special man named Jonah. Jonah was such a special man, because he was a messenger. The messages he gave were no ordinary messages. They were messages from God.

One day, God told Jonah to go to the great city of Nineveh and deliver a message. The people who lived there were living wicked lives. They were doing the most terrible things. God told Jonah to tell the people of Nineveh that they must change their ways, or their whole city would be destroyed!

Jonah was very scared to take this message to Nineveh, so he decided to run away. He got on a ship that was sailing far, far away – **he was trying to run away from God.** Once he was on the ship, Jonah went downstairs. He lay down and fell into a deep, deep sleep.

Then, God sent a massive storm with rain, thunder and lightning. The waves of the sea grew bigger and bigger and all the sailors were worried that the ship would sink! The sailors were afraid and cried out to their own gods, asking for help. And where was Jonah during this storm? He was still asleep in his cabin. The ship's captain woke Jonah up and told him to pray to his own God for help with the dangerous storm.

But Jonah knew that praying to God would not help. God had sent the storm because Jonah was running away. 'Pick me up and throw me into the sea,' he told the sailors, 'and it will become calm. This storm is my fault.'

The sailors certainly did not want to throw Jonah into the dangerous sea, so they tried to row back to dry land instead, but the storm would not stop and the sailors could not row. In the end, they had to throw Jonah overboard.

At once, the storm stopped. There was no more rain. The thunder and lightning disappeared and the waves died down. Next, God sent a fish. It was a huge fish. So large, that **it swallowed Jonah whole!**

When he was in the belly of the fish, Jonah prayed to God. He thanked God for keeping him alive and saving him from the storm and sea. Jonah was in the fish for three days and three nights. Then, at God's command, the fish spat him out onto a beach.

Jonah was given a second chance, because once again God told him to go to Nineveh and give the message. **This time, Jonah did what God told him to do.**

The people of Nineveh listened to Jonah and were very worried. **They changed their wicked ways and were good.** They even stopped eating and drinking for a time and wore special cloth to show how sorry they were. **God did not destroy Nineveh.** He did not destroy Nineveh because he saw how well the people behaved after receiving Jonah's message.

Note for the teacher: Phrases and sentences in coloured print are suggested points in the story for discussion of action, characters' feelings and atmosphere leading to musical activity.

How do Jewish people think we can 'mend the world'?

7–9

Background knowledge for teachers

Social justice is of key importance in contemporary Judaism. The Hebrew phrase *tikkun olam* is used, meaning 'healing or mending the world'. This connects well with another important Jewish belief in charitable giving. The Hebrew word for this is *tzedekah*, which is linked to justice. They also emphasise *gemilut chassidim* (acts of loving kindness). For many Jewish people, life is less about believing certain things and more about *living*, about *being* Jewish.

Rabbi Jonathan Sacks sums it up like this:

'Each faith has its unique contribution to make to the human enterprise. If I were to summarise Judaism's I would say that it lies not in climbing to heaven, but in bringing heaven down to earth. Judaism is the epiphany of everyday life.'

This unit explores ways in which Jewish people might bring 'heaven to earth', giving opportunities to pupils to consider the ways in which our world needs healing and mending, and the actions they might take in that process.

Essential knowledge for pupils

Pupils should know:

- Jewish people believe that part of being Jewish is to take some responsibility for the state our world is in and, where possible, do something to make it better
- Jewish charities like Tzedek try to put these beliefs into practice in lots of different ways, including working to protect and support children
- we all live in one world, and all have a responsibility to each other, which should include taking action, and making a contribution to 'healing the world', however small.

Assessment for Learning

This section shows some of the outcomes achievable by pupils of different abilities in the 7–9 age range.

Level	Description of achievement: I can ...
2 Almost all pupils in this age group	- say why Jewish people try to help others - talk about how I show that other people matter to me.
3 Many pupils in this age group	- describe three things a Jewish person might do to bring justice or to 'heal the world', using examples - make links between how I help others and why, and how and why some Jewish people work for justice.
4 The most able pupils in this age group	- show that I understand how following the idea of *tikkun olam* can make a real difference to how a Jewish person lives - compare different ideas about helping others, including rights for children, *tzedekah* and my own ideas.

This unit helps pupils in Scotland to achieve RME 1-05a, RME 2-05c and RME 1-06b.

Web support

Excellent and extensive resources from Tzedek:

See: tzedek.org.uk/wp-content/uploads/Tu-Bishvat-KS1-Final-April-2013.pdf

See: tzedek.org.uk/wp-content/uploads/Pesach-KS2-Final-April-2013-.pdf

Some examples of 'random acts of kindness':

See: www.randomactsofkindness.org/kindness-ideas

Subscribers and members can also download the following from the RE Today website:

- A pdf of the two quotations on p.15
- A PowerPoint presentation to support this unit.

Activity 1: Getting started: healing and mending

Show pupils some images of injuries to people (e.g. a cut finger, perhaps – nothing too terrible!) and a piece of broken furniture. Talk about what needs to happen. What could someone do to make things better? Is the furniture past saving? Would you just throw it away? Some pictures are available to help the discussion on p.16.

You might be able to help put cream on the cut, and a plaster; a doctor could re-set the arm and put a plaster cast on; essentially the body would heal itself. That won't happen with the furniture – it needs someone to do the mending or repairing!

Are there some pictures of broken things that look as if no one could mend them, and yet they are mended? What do pupils think about these?

Activity 2: Tikkun olam: healing and mending the world

Explain to pupils that Jewish teaching includes a phrase, *tikkun olam*, which means to heal or mend the world. It is one of the duties of being Jewish. Give small groups of pupils a picture of a 'broken' world and some sticky notes. Get them to talk about ways in which the world might be described as 'broken', noting down their ideas, one per sticky note.

Talk about their ideas. Put five headings on five large sheets of paper around the room: our world, our country, our town, at school, at home. As they talk, get pupils to put their sticky notes on the paper under the appropriate headings.

Note: Teachers need to be aware of and sensitive to the feelings of any pupils who may have difficult circumstances at home

Activity 3: Going further: United Nations Convention on the Rights of the Child (UNCRC)

The UNCRC outlines 42 Articles for the protection of children and childhood. Many schools are already 'rights respecting' schools, and it is worth focusing on the plight of children around the world as part of your exploration of 'mending the world'.

Page 16 outlines five of the UNCRC Articles. Give each one to a small group of pupils. Ask them to talk about what it means and give some examples of when these rights are broken.

See if any of the Articles match the earlier ideas from pupils about the 'broken world'. They will come back and look at these ideas again later.

Activity 4: Can we heal the world?

Ask the pupils: 'Can we heal or mend the world?! It seems like a big job! Is it possible?'

Show pupils the two quotations on p.15 or on the resource sheet offered as a separate download for members. Read them together; talk about any words they are unsure about.

Ask pupils:

What do Lisa Kassapian and Rabbi Sacks mean?

You might use these ideas to explore further:

- Rabbi Sacks describes the change from a broken world to a whole one. Using the ideas the class already has, get them to describe what the world would be like after healing or mending. Contrast the before and after. What would it be like to be in a mended world?

- Rabbi Sacks also talks about mending the world 'a day at a time, an act at a time'. Talk about the difference between the big problems for 'our world', and then 'zoom in' on the ones that are within reach, locally, at school, at home. Collect some examples of what pupils and others already do.

- Is there any difference between healing the world and mending it? Are there some things that would get better if we just set up the right situations (e.g. an environmental problem may be 'healed' by not cutting down more of the Amazon rainforest)? Are there some things that we have to do to mend things (e.g. relationships between people in areas of war)?

Activity 5: How do people try to 'heal the world'?

Ask pupils to explore the case studies on p.17. How are these helping to 'heal the world'? Which of the UNCRC Articles are they addressing? Ask pupils to do a 'before and after' analysis again: describe the 'broken' world before these charities do their work, and then the 'healed or mended' world afterwards. What else needs to be done? How far are these charities 'bringing heaven to earth'?

Ask pupils to imagine an award for 'the best mend-the-world work'. Ask some of the more able pupils to present a short speech as to why their case study example should win the Award. The class can vote, giving reasons for their choice.

Activity 6: Tu B'shevat: Jewish New Year for trees

Take your pupils outside. If there are trees nearby, get pupils to lie underneath them (health and safety and bird droppings permitting, of course!) and look up. Listen to the wind through the leaves, to the birds. Think about what size of seed these trees came from. Imagine all that energy contained within a tiny seed! All that life, that growth, the trunks, the twigs, the buds, leaves, flowers and fruit – all growing from that tiny seed! Pushing downwards, sucking up water and minerals from the deep earth; reaching upwards, seeking the sunlight – producing flowers and fruit!

Ask pupils for their responses to this experience. They might write a poem in an outline of a tree, or plant a seedling in the school garden!

Introduce them to the Jewish festival of Tu B'shevat, or New Year for trees, using the information on p.18. Talk about how this fits in with the idea of tikkun olam.

Activity 7: Random acts of kindness: applying the lesson

You might copy the Jewish practice of gemilut chassidim (acts of loving kindness) by getting your pupils to think about what kind things they could do for others. See if they can think of some that will help to heal the world. Run a 'Random Acts of Kindness' week – and challenge them to try and carry out some acts of kindness, explaining why they are doing it, making links to the Jewish idea of **tikkun olam**.

Clean up after yourself!	Give away a toy.	Listen to a friend.
Weed a flowerbed.	Bake someone a cake.	Ask about someone's beliefs.
Make a bird feeder.	Say thank you with a letter.	Use less water.

> We (Jews) are here to make a difference, to mend the fractures of the world, a day at a time, an act at a time, for as long as it takes to make it a place of justice and compassion where the lonely are not alone, the poor not without help; where the cry of the vulnerable is heeded and those who are wronged are heard.
>
> Rabbi Jonathan Sacks, *To Heal a Fractured World: The Ethics of Responsibility*, Bloomsbury 2005.

> Social justice is very important in British Judaism. It is called 'tikkun olam' which means repairing or mending the world. Helping those who are treated unfairly is really important as it provides hope for the future. In Judaism, giving to the poor is considered to be an act of justice and fairness. Jewish people do not think the world should be the way that it is. They hope and pray that they can change it.
>
> Lisa Kassapian

Activity 1 — Healing and mending

What is happening in these photos?

© Kondor83 - Fotolia.com

What is the difference between those pictures and these?

Activity 2

Tikkun olam: healing and mending the world

In what ways is our world 'broken'?

© Nikita Kuzmenkov - Fotolia.com

Activity 3 — United Nations Convention on the Rights of the Child

Article 14
Children have the right to think and believe what they want and to practise their religion, as long as they are not stopping other people from enjoying their rights. Parents should guide their children on these matters.

Article 23
Children who have any kind of disability should have special care and support so that they can lead full and independent lives.

Article 24
Children have the right to good quality health care and to clean water, nutritious food and a clean environment so that they will stay healthy. Rich countries should help poorer countries achieve this.

Article 31
All children have a right to relax and play, and to join in a wide range of activities.

Article 32
The Government should protect children from work that is dangerous or might harm their health or their education.

Case studies: ways of healing the world

Tzedek

Tzedek supports BREAD, a local group in West Bengal, India, to train young people to improve their lives and earn a decent wage.

Many young people in India have to leave primary school to earn money so that their families can survive. BREAD (Bureau of Rural Economical and Agriculture Development) has helped over 120 boys and 280 girls to earn a living by helping them to learn skills such as embroidery and diesel pump repairs.

Sharwan comes from a poor lower-caste family in Bihar, India. He went on Tzedek's training through BREAD, learning how to mend electric motors. His earnings have improved from £11 to £94 per month. Now he can support himself and pay for his younger brothers and sisters to attend school.

Tzedek's 'School for Life' programme is making a difference to the education of around 40,000 primary school children in Ghana, Africa.

Without the basics – reading and writing – pupils cannot continue on to secondary level education.

Unfortunately thousands of children are held back by poor education. Many adults in Ghana cannot read or write. By teaching children living in poverty to read and write, they can be helped out of a lifetime of struggle, malnutrition and poor health, and be given the chance to make a success of their lives and help to transform their nation.

The project has trained over 900 teachers to help the children to learn better. Better learning means better lives!

Oasis of Peace UK
British Friends of Neve Shalom / Wahat al-Salam

واحة السلام
נווה שלום

Registered Charity No. 290062

The founders of the UK charity **Jewish Child's Day** believe that no child should live in poverty, need or suffering – anywhere. The charity supports other charities helping disabled Jewish children, as well as those who are poor or abandoned.

For example, **Step-by-Step** gives disabled Jewish children in the UK the chance to take part in riding, ice skating, football, cycling, swimming and hydrotherapy after school. These activities can help the physical and emotional health of these children.

Cosgrove Care is based in Glasgow, Scotland, and provides care for children with learning disabilities from the age of three upwards. They support children in their own home and through a range of out-of-school leisure and sport activities, including water play, drama, music, arts and crafts, cooking and baking, sports, construction and a selection of outings.

Oasis of Peace is the English translation of the name of Neve Shalom (Hebrew)/Wahat al-Salam (Arabic).

It is situated in Israel, midway between Tel Aviv and Jerusalem. It is a community where Jewish and Palestinian Arab Israeli citizens have lived together in peace for the past 40 years.

Together, they teach their children in both languages about each other's cultures, religions and traditions. It is a model for peace and harmony between people.

See: www.oasisofpeace.org.uk/

Tu B'shevat: New Year for Trees!

Tu B'shevat

Every year, many Jewish people celebrate Tu B'shevat – New Year for Trees. It takes place on the 15th day of the Jewish month of Shvat (in 2015 this is 4 February). It reminds Jewish people of the importance of the land – specifically the land of Israel. This festival of love for trees reminds them of their story as a people who lived off the land.

Jewish people often celebrate the festival by planting trees and eating fruit. Many customs surround the eating of fruit on Tu B'shevat. These include trying to eat fruits particularly associated with Israel, such as grapes, figs, pomegranates, olives and dates or eating a fruit which you have not yet eaten that year. Some Jews will take part in a Tu B'shevat seder. In some ways, this is similar to a seder meal at Passover, but the focus is on the fruits of the tree and discussing philosophical ideas related to Tu B'shevat.

Sacred text

Jewish people are inspired during this festival by texts from Jewish writings:

> The Holy One, blessed be He, occupied Himself with planting immediately after Creation of the world. For it is specifically written: 'And the Lord G-d planted a garden in Eden'. So shall you also, when you enter the land of Israel, first of all occupy yourself in planting.
>
> Vayikra Rabba, 25

> For the Lord G-d will lead you into the good land, a land flowing with waters ... A land of wheat and barley and vine, of fig and pomegranate, the land of the olive and honey.
>
> Megillat Esther, 9:22

Lessons to learn

There are lessons that can be learned from trees:

> Whoever has more wisdom than deeds is like a tree with many branches but few roots, and the wind shall tear him from the ground ... Whoever has more deeds than wisdom is like a tree with more roots than branches, and no hurricane will uproot him from the spot.
>
> Mishnah, Tractate Avot, Ch.3, Mishnah 17

A story shared at Tu B'shevat

> A wise rabbi was walking along a road when he saw a man planting a tree. The rabbi asked him, 'How many years will it take for this tree to bear fruit?'
>
> The man answered that it would take seventy years.
>
> The rabbi asked, 'Are you so fit and strong that you expect to live that long and eat its fruit?'
>
> The man answered, 'I found a fruitful world because my forefathers planted for me. So I will do the same for my children.'
>
> The Midrash

Why does Zara give money away at Ramadan?

8–11

Background knowledge for teachers

The month of Ramadan (the ninth month in the Islamic calendar) has special religious significance. In this month every adult Muslim fasts from dawn until sunset. Ramadan is an opportunity to increase one's God consciousness, or 'taqwa'; it is regarded as a time of spiritual discipline that contributes to spiritual growth. There is also a sense of identifying with the poor, and encouraging Muslims to think about the weak and needy. This is also the time of the year that Muslims are obliged to give a proportion of their income to those less fortunate than themselves. Muslims give 2.5 per cent of their surplus wealth to charity. Surplus wealth is things like your savings and your gold and silver jewellery.

This unit supports pupils enquiring into why Muslims choose to give Zakat, using a mystery activity, and also expects them to be able to extract key information to understand the Islamic practice. There are then differentiated opportunities to use their knowledge to consider what Muslims might choose to do with their money.

The tasks have been written clearly showing how they can be adapted for different ages and abilities of pupils.

Assessment for Learning

This section shows some of the outcomes achievable by pupils of different abilities in the 8–11 age range.

Level	Description of achievement: I can …
3 Almost all pupils in this age group	• make a link between the giving of Zakat and fasting in Ramadan • describe what Zakat is and why it is important to Muslims • suggest answers Muslims might give to questions about Zakat.
4 Many pupils in this age group	• describe why Muslims give Zakat and how Muslims believe it is different to ordinary charitable giving • refer to Islamic sources or practices when explaining why giving Zakat is a 'pillar of Islam'.
5 The most able pupils in this age group	• explain the impact of the ways that Muslim charities like Muslim Hands or Islamic Relief put religious teaching into action • express my views about the practice and impact of Zakat, relating the ideas to my own life.

This unit helps pupils in Scotland to achieve RME 2-05b and RME 2-06c.

Essential knowledge for pupils

Pupils should know:

- that Zakat is an obligatory practice for Muslims
- why Muslims practice Zakat
- that Zakat is usually given in Ramadan
- that the giving of Zakat is a form of worship for Muslims. Muslims believe giving Zakat helps the person who gives it as much as the person who receives it.

Web support

Further information on Zakat can be found on the websites of the two charities used in this unit:

See: www.muslimhands.org.uk
See: www.nzf.org.uk

Subscribers and members can also download the following from the RE Today website: www.retoday.org.uk

- A set of the cards for the mystery on pp. 21–2
- Quotations for Activity 1.

Links across the curriculum

English: This work connects to Literacy and the English curriculum, providing ideas for reasoned speaking, listening and debating.

RE Today Services

19

Activity 1: Using your money

Many pupils are given money over which they have some control – pocket money. This opening activity encourages the children to think about how they use any money that they get.

Ask the pupils to work in pairs and write a statement or draw a picture about what they do with any pocket money they get. Give each pair a copy of one the statements from George or Francesca, as shown below. These statements are available for REToday subscribers and NATRE members to download from our website.

Ask the pairs to compare the statements.

- Is the money used for similar or different things?
- What is positive about the way the money is used? Why is it positive?
- Could the money be used in a better way?

Ask the pair to meet up with another pair who looked at a different statement. Ask them to share and compare their responses and ideas.

I get £8 per month, I don't really think about what I spend it on. Sometimes I buy things for me or presents for my mum, sometimes I might give it to charity like when it is Remembrance Sunday or Comic Relief.

George, 8

I get £5 pocket money per month. I organise it so I have £2 to spend, £2 to save and £1 goes in my charity money box. I use it for lots of things like buying cakes for Children in Need or sponsoring people.

Francesca, 10

Activity 2: A mystery: why does Zara give money away at Ramadan?

In advance of the lesson, print the statements needed for the mystery on pp. 21 and 22, including the key question, and prepare enough packs for one for each group of 3–4 pupils.

The cards have been prepared so you can differentiate the learning. One way of differentiating the cards is to use different cards for different groups.

For younger or less able pupils use 1, 2, 4, 5, 7, 9, 10, 11, 12, 13, 15, 17, 18, 19.

For older or more able pupils use all of the cards.

Explain to pupils that they will be given a question to answer, and a series of clues.

The task is to identify what they think is a sound answer to the question, based on the clues they are provided with. Point out to pupils that it is the quality of their thinking that is important in the activity, not necessarily a 'right' answer.

Working in groups of 3–4, pupils:

- Empty their card pack, and identify the central question which they have to answer. This should remain visible at all times, as a guide and prompt to thinking.
- Study the 'clues' on the cards and move them around the table, discussing, deciding, explaining, refining their ideas as part of the thinking process. Pupils work to find a plausible answer to the question.
- Respond to the teacher, who mediates to encourage pupils to justify the reasons for their views as they emerge during the activity.
- Contribute to a whole class discussion on what they think the answer to the question is and how they can justify their answer. Which information was most useful and which was a red herring?

Activity 3: Knowledge collection

Arrange the pupils to work in pairs and set them the challenge of creating a Zakat Top Ten of facts that they know. They could even compile a Zakat quiz for another pair to complete.

A mystery: Why does Zara give money away at Ramadan?

1. Each month Zara gives some of her money away to charity, for instance she sponsors a child in another country through the charity Plan.org

2. *[Islamic Relief advertisement: "He'll either be begging or thanking God. THIS RAMADAN YOU CAN DECIDE. CALL 0800 520 0000" – www.islamic-relief.org.uk]*

3. The word Zakat means 'purification', or making something clean.

4. Zara says, 'We like to give Zakat because we get the feel of how it is for poor people, it makes you grateful for what you have. Thinking about people who are less fortunate than you should be a big focus of Ramadan.'

5. *[Photograph of a couple working out their Zakat]*

6. Zakat is obligatory – it has to be given. Muslims work out how much they have to give. They give 2.5% of their surplus wealth. Surplus wealth is things like your savings and your gold and silver jewellery. Therefore if you have £10,000 of wealth liable to Zakat, you would pay £250.

7. Giving Zakat is an act of worship.

8. Giving Zakat helps the person who gives as much as the person who receives.

9. Ramadan is the ninth month of the Islamic calendar.

10. Last year Zara's friend Adam gave £200 as Zakat during Ramadan.

11. The more money you have got, the more money you give as Zakat.

12. Zara is a Muslim woman living in Birmingham.

RE Today Services — Photocopiable by purchasing institutions

A mystery: Why does Zara give money away at Ramadan?

13 'When you give money away, you're not thinking, "I could have spent that." You are thinking, "Allah has been good to me." It makes you thankful.'

14 When a baby is born into an Islamic family, a small amount of gold is given on their behalf. From the beginning of their lives, a Muslim is someone who gives to others.

15 Eid-ul-Adha is not just a party to celebrate the end of fasting, it is a big opportunity to share money and food with the whole community. Even when they are having fun, Muslims should be charitable.

16 He is not a believer who eats while his neighbour remains hungry by his side.
Hadith

17 Zara says 'I fast to remember people in poverty in this country and in poorer countries; it helps me think about how I can help by giving money. I am really thankful to God that I can give Zakat.'

18 Adam gives some of his Zakat money to Islamic Relief, a big charity which uses Zakat money to help those who are needy all over the world.

19 Zakat is compulsory for those who have surplus wealth.

20 Muslims have to wait for the sighting of the new moon before they know when Eid will start.

21 Muslims wash before they pray. This shows they want to be spiritually clean before praying to Allah.

22 Zara and her family break their fast with prayers and by eating dates. They do this every evening in Ramadan.

23 The Prophet Muhammad said:
'Every single day, each person has two angels near him who have descended from heaven. The one says, "O Allah, compensate the person who gives to charity," the other says, "O Allah, inflict a loss on the person who withholds his money."'
Hadith

24 Zakat funds should be given to people who fit the following categories:
- Someone who has no job or possessions.
- Someone who has a job but not enough to meet his basic needs.
- Someone who has converted to Islam.
- Someone who has had to borrow money to meet their basic needs.
- Someone who is a slave.
- Someone who promotes things that are good in the eyes of Allah.
- Someone who is stranded on a journey.
- Someone who helps to collects Zakat, if they need help.

National Zakat Foundation

See: www.nzf.org.uk

The National Zakat Foundation uses Zakat funds and voluntary donations collected in the United Kingdom for the benefit of local people in need. They support Muslim people in towns and cities across the country, including widows, orphans, refugees, the elderly as well as the homeless.

The story of Bilal – helped by Zakat funds.

See: www.nzf.org.uk/OurWork/Bilal

Last year a large supermarket worked with the National Zakat Foundation to help them to collect extra money to help people in need.

Muslim Hands

See: www.muslimhands.org.uk

This British charity that started in Nottingham in 1993 is dedicated to serving the most vulnerable people across the world by addressing the root causes of poverty and supporting communities working to improve their own lives.

Operating in countries across four continents they work to make a long-term difference, for example improving education, and also in emergency situations such as natural disasters.

See some details of their work on their website:

Clean water: http://muslimhands.org.uk/our-work/water/

Sponsoring an orphan: http://muslimhands.org.uk/giving/orphan-sponsorship/

Children living on the streets: http://muslimhands.org.uk/campaigns/2014/street-children/

I am so thankful that I can give Zakat each year – it helps me become closer to Allah. It is also a reminder that the money I have is not all for me, I must share it with those who need it more than me.

Zara is a married Muslim woman in her 30s. She works hard all year and sees Ramadan as a time to give something to others.

When I give Zakat I talk to my husband about it but it is my decision what to do with the Zakat money I donate.

Which charities should I support this year? There are so many people in need!

Activity 4 — Zakat donations

This activity will suit younger or less able pupils.

Share the information about the two Muslim charities shown on p.23 with the pupils. Remind them about Zara and explain that today it is their task to help her to decide who to donate to. There are web links that you might want to look at as a class.

Ask the pupils to imagine they work for either the National Zakat Foundation or Muslim Hands and have been asked to create a poster to display in either a mosque, a station or other public place. The poster needs to show clearly what the charity will do with the money they receive but also use persuasive text so that someone like Zara will think about donating.

The poster should include

- Who the charity supports
- An eye-catching picture

If older or more able pupils are completing this task they should include some information about how this charity is an appropriate place to donate Zakat funds.

Activity 5 — Pitching the charity

This activity will suit older or more able pupils.

This activity can be completed after Activity 4 or as an alternative, more challenging activity.

Arrange the pupils into groups of three or four. Ask the pupils to imagine they work for either National Zakat Foundation or Muslim Hands. The information and web links on p.23 will support them in this task.

They are going to a meeting where there will be lots of people who want some ideas about how to spend their Zakat giving. In the meeting they will have two minutes to give some information about the importance of Zakat, their charity and why people in the audience should donate some of their Zakat funds to them.

After the pupils have written and practised their presentations you could play the role of Zara. In your role you should hear the pitches and explain which has been more informative and persuasive.

Support pupils with sentence starters like the ones below to help them to know what to include in their pitches. Remind pupils to use the knowledge gained during the mystery activity as they create their presentations.

'Zakat is important for Muslims because …'

'Our charity is an appropriate place to donate Zakat funds because …'

Deciding what to do with the Zakat money

9–11

Eight sentences for a happy world: the Beatitudes of Jesus

Background knowledge for teachers

Many religions encourage the pursuit of justice, peace, pure-heartedness and mercy. In Christian scripture Jesus begins his life as a rabbi with the 'Sermon on the Mount'. At the very beginning of his work, he teaches his followers 'eight sentences to change the world'. These sentences proclaim eight blessings on people who seek to live their lives in particular ways. It is fair to say that they are widely recognised as a piece of spiritual genius. The Beatitudes are not simple, and in this chapter of the book we have not plumbed their depths. This work is a simple introduction to some 'deep stuff'.

This work uses some simple versions of the Beatitudes, and sets four learning activities to build understanding and application: children will use their growing knowledge to communicate ideas through considering what makes us happy; through cartoons; through an example of a Christian charitable project in Ethiopia of the ways Christians co-operate globally and locally; and through applying the Beatitudes for themselves.

These approaches are intended to build up understanding and insight by revisiting some profound key concepts in different ways.

Essential knowledge for pupils

Pupils should know:
- some key words such as blessed, Bible, Gospel, Beatitudes, justice, mercy
- how and why Christians try to put the teaching of Jesus into action.

Links across the curriculum

English: This work connects to Literacy and the English curriculum, providing ideas for reasoned speaking, listening and debating.

Geography: Studying the story from Ethiopia meets learning objectives for Geography, enabling pupils to describe and understand the distribution of natural resources.

PSHE and wellbeing: Pupils will consider happiness and the ways in which people seek happiness.

Thinking skills: Activities like '32-Sentence Knockout' enable pupils to rank, sort and analyse different ideas.

Assessment for Learning

This section shows some of the outcomes achievable by pupils of different abilities in the 9–11 age range.

Level	Description of achievement: I can …
3 Almost all pupils in this age group	• describe simply what Jesus taught his followers in the Beatitudes • make links between 'ancient wisdom' and modern life, talking thoughtfully about what makes us happy • give a simple reaction to one or more of Jesus' sayings, asking my own good questions about what makes us happy.
4 Many pupils in this age group	• use words like blessing, beatitudes, and justice to show I understand some meanings of Jesus' teaching • show my understanding of Jesus' ideas about blessings and happiness, in a cartoon, discussion or piece of writing • apply ideas from the Beatitudes to a story of Christian action in the contemporary world.
5 The most able pupils in this age group	• explain what some of the Beatitudes mean, giving examples • explain why the 'eight sentences' of the Beatitudes are important for Christian people, giving reasons for my own ideas • express my own ideas and views about 'the way to happiness' in the light of the learning from religion I have been doing.

This unit helps pupils in Scotland to achieve RME 2-01b, RME 2-01c and RME 2-02b .

Web support

Look at the website of SUNARMA, the Ethiopian Partner of the Methodist Relief and Development Fund to find about more about their work.

See: www.sunarma.org/Success-Stories/

Subscribers and members can also download the following from the RE Today website: www.retoday.org.uk

- A PowerPoint presentation to support the unit of work
- A copy of the 32-Sentence Knockout on p.27.
- A 32 – team elimination chart.

Activity 1: '32 Sentence Knockout'

This thinking skills idea uses dialogue to help a class refine their ideas by making agreed choices. They work on a 'sentence knockout', deciding which sentence wins as a description of what makes you happy.

The 'knockout' activity works like a sports draw: each of the sentences is 'drawn against' one other, and pupils decide by discussion which one is most likely to make us happy. That one goes through to the next round. By the time you get to the quarter finals, semis and final, the sentences left will probably include some which make major contributions to happiness. There is a set of 32 on p.27 (and in a PDF for members and subscribers on the website).

A great way to run the activity is to put the sentences in two sections of 16 at each end of a wall (see the diagram on p.27), and have the pupils discuss in half-class groups which one 'wins' each heat. They can vote after several people have said what they think. Then there will be a 'final' between the two half classes. Another way to do this is to lay the sentences out on the floor in the middle of a 'circle time' discussion.

Activity 2: Making sense of Jesus' 'eight sentences to change the world'

Remind the class of their '32 Sentence Knockout'.
- What did they think makes people happy, most of all?

Ask pupils to take some cards and felt-tipped pens and write onto them the phrase 'You are happy if…' Complete the sentences in original, detailed and deep ways, and share the results. Pupils can do two or three each if they like, but 'deep' matters more than 'quick' here. Ask pupils if they would like to see Jesus' answer to this activity. Tell them it is hard to understand in some ways, so we have a 'main version' and a simple version.

Give groups of three or four the Bible text of Matthew 5:1-10 from p.28 in the centre of a sheet of paper and ask the groups to annotate it around the edges with questions about the meaning and ideas of what Jesus said. Then swap papers. Ask the new groups to read the simplified version of the beatitudes from p.28, and see if they can suggest answers to the questions the first group have raised.

In whole class discussion, consider together any parts of the text where the meaning is not clear.

Activity 3: Happiness cartoons

Give pairs of pupils a copy of p.29, and show the pictures in colour on the whiteboard, or use the PowerPoint presentation at www.retoday.org.uk for members and subscribers.

Ask pupils to:
- discuss with a talk partner three good things about each cartoon
- agree with their talk partner which cartoon is best and why
- work on their own to make a cartoon or drawing of one of Jesus' eight Beatitudes, and explain how it shows its true meaning.

Arrange a classroom display of the work.

Invite a Christian person, perhaps a minister or priest from your local church, to come and see the work, and ask them for comments about the meaning of the eight sayings.

Activity 4: The work of the MRDF: honey, money and being blessed

Pupils' learning about Jesus' 'eight sentences for happiness' needs to enable them to apply ideas for themselves.

Arrange pupils into groups of three or four.
- Give each group p.30 in cut up into six cards
- Ask them to work out the right order for the story.

Read the story aloud together as a class.
- How many people are in the story?
- What does each one do?
- How are they connected?

Each of the six boxes in the story has a question at the end. Can pupils, in small groups, create answers to these six questions? These quotes may help:

> "Kindu lends out his Queen Bee. Maybe that shows that he has a pure heart."

> "The whole point of SUNARMA is longing for justice."

> "Blessed are the merciful' - it tells you that if give to charity, showing mercy, you will be blessed."

> "In a way, Danny's gift made peace for Kindu."

32 Sentence knockout: You are happy if. . .

You are happy if you are loved.	You are happy if you have a friend.	You are happy if school is over.	You are happy if you have no worries.
You are happy if there is peace in your country.	You are happy if your family is together.	You are happy if there is chocolate in your hand.	You are happy if you have plenty of money.
You are happy if you are helping someone else.	You are happy if you have love in your life.	You are happy if you are safe.	You are happy if nothing scares you.
You are happy if you get the joke.	You are happy if you can forget tomorrow and yesterday.	You are happy if you feel God near you.	You are happy if you don't expect much.
You are happy if the sun shines on you.	You are happy if you don't let the rain get to you.	You are happy if you are together with your mates.	You are happy if you are together with your family.
You are happy if you feel thankful, and say it!	You are happy if your pet loves you.	You are happy if you make peace in your life.	You are happy if you have a new games console and phone.
You are happy if you know your mum loves you.	You are happy if you are dancing to your favourite song.	You are happy if you forget your troubles.	You are happy if you take time to notice the beauty of the earth.
You are happy if your pray.	You are happy if you win.	You are happy if you are loved by God.	You are happy if you can be alone but never lonely.

An elimination diagram for 32 entries is available for subscribers and NATRE members to download from www.retoday.org.uk

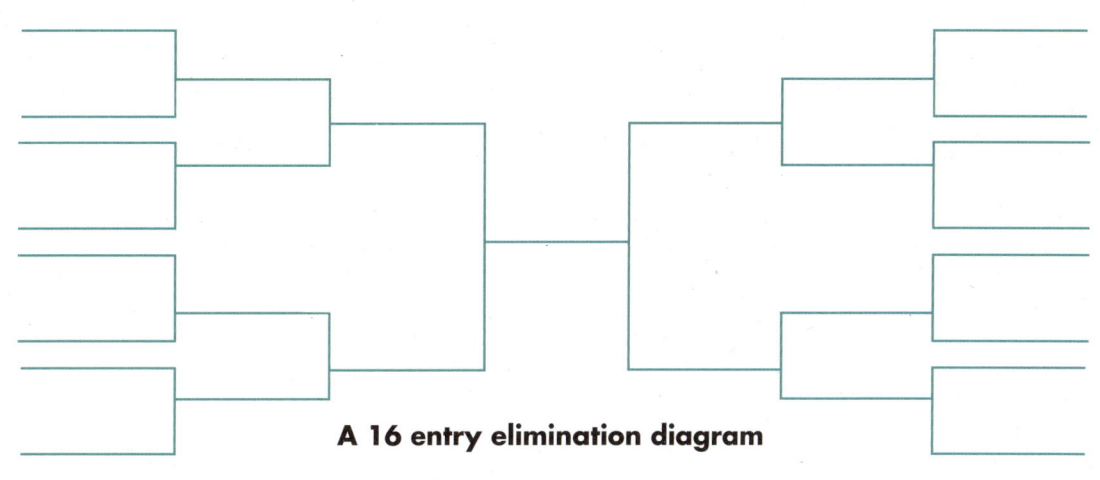

A 16 entry elimination diagram

Jesus' way to happiness: the Bible text from Matthew 5 and a simplified version

Jesus' eight sentences for a happier life: the Beatitudes	A simplified version of the Beatitudes
Blessed are the poor in spirit, for theirs is the kingdom of heaven.	You are happy if you rely on God, not yourself. God's kingdom belongs to you.
Blessed are those who mourn, for they will be comforted.	You are happy if you wish things were better. You will be comforted.
Blessed are the meek, for they will inherit the earth.	You are happy if you think you are low down. God will give you all the Earth
Blessed are those who hunger and thirst for righteousness, for they will be filled.	You are happy if you long for justice. One day you will be satisfied.
Blessed are the merciful, for they will receive mercy.	You are happy if you are full of mercy. Others will then show mercy to you.
Blessed are the pure in heart, for they will see God.	You are happy if your heart is pure. You will see God.
Blessed are the peacemakers, for they will be called children of God.	You are happy if you make peace. You will be known as a child of God.
Blessed are those who are persecuted for righteousness' sake, for theirs is the kingdom of heaven.	You are happy if you are picked on for doing good. God's kingdom belongs to you.

Matthew 5:1-10 (NRSV)

Happiness cartoons

You have been thinking about our roads to happiness, and you have done some work on what Jesus taught his followers in the Bible.

Here are three cartoons by pupils aged 9 and 10, in which they take one of Jesus' sayings in a simple version and try to show in their cartoons what it means.

- Talk with your partner about these three.
- Notice three good things about each cartoon, and agree – if you can – which one you like best.

Now work on your own

- Choose one of Jesus' eight Beatitudes and make a cartoon or drawing of your own that shows its true meaning.

Be happy when your heart is right with God, because it is then that you will see that God is at work in the world around you.

Be happy when others treat you badly because you follow god, because your reward will be great in heaven.

Be happy with what you have because then you will find your heavenly father provides everything

The eight sentences in action

Can you see how Jesus' teaching makes sense of this story from Ethiopia?

Sweet success in Ethiopia

Kindu is a 48-year-old dad from Ethiopia. He has two children with his wife and they adopted another boy too.

Years ago, he learned to keep bees and make honey for sale, to get a little money and feed the family. But Ethiopia is a poor country. Kindu's district of Dibele used to be full of trees, but people cut the wood to sell, and the soil became rocky and dusty. Things didn't grow so well. Life was hard.

What could help Kindu and his family?

SURNAMA gave money for training to bee keepers

The charity SUNARMA works all over Ethiopia to help people who are poor. It doesn't just give out food. SUNARMA helps people to look after themselves. It's a 'hand up', not a 'hand out'.

When they found out that Kindu was keeping bees, they helped him by showing him a new kind of hive and they helped him to breed some stronger bees as well. He learned to use his queen bee to breed better.

Why might this be better than just giving Kindu's family some money?

Not just bees! Trees and water too!

SUNARMA has been trying to make the land more fruitful in Dibele. More trees make a big difference, so they have planted over a million saplings!

Another way to help is build a water channel so that water flows to where it will help crops grow. Then farmers can get two harvests a year instead of just one. Two hundred and fifty people in one community each gave what they could: rocks, land, a few days' work, all co-operating to build the new water channel. Now they enjoy water all year round flowing to their fields.

What links are there between honey, money, Jesus, Danny, Kindu, water, justice, peace and trees?

Harvest: time to say thank you

Danny, aged 10, went to his church in Wigan one Sunday in October. His mum gave him a bag of apples and some honey to take. 'Why am I taking these?' he asked. 'It's Harvest' said mum. 'There will be a sale of gifts, so we can help people who are in need.'

Churches in Britain send money to the Methodist Relief and Development Fund (MRDF) at harvest time. It is a time for Christians to thank God for the goodness of the earth. One way to do this is to help those with too little to eat. Another way is to help people to work for their own futures to help themselves and their families. Danny's gift was sold, and the money was sent to SUNARMA by MRDF.

Do little actions make peace, or help justice along?

More honey and being a good neighbour too!

More honey and being a good neighbour too!

After going on a SUNARMA training course, Kindu became a better honey famer. He says:

> 'From the training I learnt how to choose better breeds of bees and how to manage the bees. I also got two modern beehives. Now I am gaining the honey! I have learnt to breed with the queen bee so now I can also 'lend her out' to other farmers who are my neighbours. They can also breed bees. I am very glad to be an example so that others can learn to keep bees and have this experience also.'

What kind of person do you think Kindu is?

Better beehives, more honey

Kindu says: 'When I had my old beehives, I got about 4kg of honey a year from them.' The modern beehives that SUNARMA gives to the honey farmers have three layers in them. Lots more bees live in them, and make lots more honey.

Now, says Kindu,

> 'I get about 30kg of honey every year – seven times more than before. I can sell the honey at a good profit, and use the income to buy more food and better clothes for my children.'

Which two of Jesus' 'eight sentences for a happier world' have the clearest connection to this story?

Look at the website of SUNARMA, the Ethiopian Partner of MRDF. Ask some high-achieving pupils to choose another story of their work to tell the rest of the class.

See: www.sunarma.org/Success-Stories/

Subject Leader support: fairness and justice

Where do fairness and justice fit in RE?

Children and adults are not usually slow to express their sense of injustice when they perceive themselves to be treated unfairly or unjustly. In RE we begin with fairness and encourage pupils to look beyond the injustices they may suffer and open their eyes to some of the major examples of injustice in the wider world. Religions and worldviews have plenty to say about injustice as shown in the units in this book and in sources of wisdom that religious people turn to for guidance.

Most agreed syllabuses and other RE guidance documents expect that pupils will look at beliefs in action in the world: what difference does it make to how you live your life that you hold a set of beliefs; how do you act on those beliefs? Pupils are often extremely interested in issues of fairness or justice as they can see it is relevant to the world around them and they often hold passionate ideals about the importance of concepts such as fairness, justice, peace and environmental issues. When teaching about fairness and justice it is essential to ensure that the focus remains on RE and does not focus solely on 'doing good works' or charity. In RE it is important to engage critically with what religions and worldviews do and say about fairness and justice through looking at story, sacred text and practices.

Stories of fairness and justice

There are a great many stories that illustrate the importance of justice. Many have been highlighted in this book. Further examples of stories to support learning about fairness and justice are listed below:

- The tale of the two billionaires, adapted from the Jataka tales from the Buddhist tradition. The story can be found on p.24 of the document below

See: http://learn.christianaid.org.uk/Images/thoughtfully_book_tcm16-22708.pdf

- The parable of the sheep and the goats, Matthew 25:31-36
- Zaccheus the tax collector, Luke 19:1-10
- The widow's mite, Mark 12:41-3
- Bhai Kanhaya: a Sikh story of a man who shared water with Sikh soldiers and their opponents on the battlefield.

Wise words: How can we use them?

Sources of wisdom, both sacred text and wise people from religion and worldviews, have much to say about fairness and justice. On p.32 there is a selection of quotes from sacred text and on p.33 some quotations from inspirational people as a resource for you to use when supporting teachers. Try some of these ideas:

Artistic interpretation of wisdom

Choose a quotation and stick it in the middle of a piece of paper. Ask pupils to draw a picture of what the quote means or what a situation would be like if people followed the advice or teaching in the quote.

Comparing wisdom

Give pupils a selection of the quotations from sacred texts and inspirational people. Can they cluster some that are saying the same thing? What themes can they see? Ask pupils to write about the similarities and differences between a selection of the quotes.

Diamond Nine

Give pupils the quotations on p.33. Ask them to work in pairs and choose nine quotes they would like to work with.

Arrange the quotes into a 'Diamond Nine' with the quote they agree with most at the top and the quote they agree with least at the bottom. Ask them to share their ideas and comments about the quotes with another pair.

RE Today Services

Quotations from sacred texts on fairness and justice

Christianity

Happy are those who want justice above all things, they shall see justice done.

Happy are those who risk danger to do what is right, they know what it is to live in God's kingdom.

Matthew, 5:6, 10

Let no-one seek his own good, but the good of his neighbour.

1 Corinthians 10:24

And don't forget to do good and to share with those in need. These are the sacrifices that please God.

Hebrews 13,16

For I was hungry and you gave me something to eat, I was thirsty and you gave me something to drink, I was a stranger and you invited me in, I needed clothes and you clothed me, I was sick and you looked after me, I was in prison and you came to visit me.

Matthew 25:35-36

Judaism

What does the Law require of you but to do justice, to show kindness and to walk humbly with your God.

Tenakh, Micah 6:8

This is what the law says:
Do what is fair and right.
Save from the robber who is robbed.
Do no wrong to foreigners, orphans or widows.
Commit no offence.
Do not kill innocent people.

Tenakh, Jeremiah 22:3

The world stands upon three things: upon the Law, upon worship, and upon showing kindness.

Mishnah 1.2

Learn to do what is right!
Promote justice!
Give the oppressed reason to celebrate!
Take up the cause of the orphan!
Defend the rights of the widow!

Tenakh, Isaiah 1:17

Islam

All you who believe. Stand out firmly for justice as witnesses to Allah …

Qur'an 4:135

Be mindful of your duty (to Allah), and do good works; … be mindful of your duty and believe.

Qur'an 5:93

God requires justice and kindness and giving…

Qur'an 16:90

And be steadfast in prayer and regular in charity: and whatever good ye send forth for your souls before you, ye shall find it with Allah: for Allah sees well all that ye do.

Surah 2:110

A man once asked the Prophet what was the best thing in Islam and the latter replied, 'It is to feed the hungry and to give the greeting of peace both to those one knows and to those one doesn't know'

Hadith of Bukhari

Buddhism

To avoid all evil, to cultivate good, and to cleanse one's mind – this is the teaching of the Buddhas.

Dhammapada 183

Conquer anger by love. Conquer evil by good. Conquer the stingy by giving. Conquer the liar by truth.

Dhammapada 223

Quotations from www.accesstoinsight.org.

Hinduism

Ahimsa (nonviolence) is the highest duty.

Padma Purana 1.31.27

Let your conduct be marked by truthfulness in word and deed and thought.

Taittiriya Upanishad 1.11.1

Sikhism

No-one is my enemy and no-one is a stranger. I get along with everyone.

Guru Granth Sahib p1299

Whoever has good luck written into their life can apply themselves to do seva – selfless service.

Guru Granth Sahib p1142